ORIGINAL KEYS for SINGERS

PIANO / VOCAL

# BROADWAY HITS
## FOR FEMALE SINGERS

ISBN 978-1-4803-4129-6

HAL•LEONARD®
CORPORATION
7777 W. BLUEMOUND RD. P.O. BOX 13819 MILWAUKEE, WI 53213

Visit Hal Leonard Online at
**www.halleonard.com**

# ALL I ASK OF YOU
## from THE PHANTOM OF THE OPERA

Music by ANDREW LLOYD WEBBER
Lyrics by CHARLES HART
Additional Lyrics by RICHARD STILGOE

RAOUL:
No more talk of dark-ness, for-get these wide-eyed fears: I'm here, noth-ing can harm you, my words will warm and calm you. Let me be your free-dom, let day-light dry your tears: I'm here, with you, be-side you, to

safe, no one will find you your fears are far be-hind you.

CHRISTINE: All I want is free-dom, a world with no more night; and

you, al-ways be-side me, to hold me and to hide me. RAOUL: Then

say you'll share with me one love, one life-time; let me lead you from your

# AND I AM TELLING YOU I'M NOT GOING

from DREAMGIRLS

Music by HENRY KRIEGER
Lyric by TOM EYEN

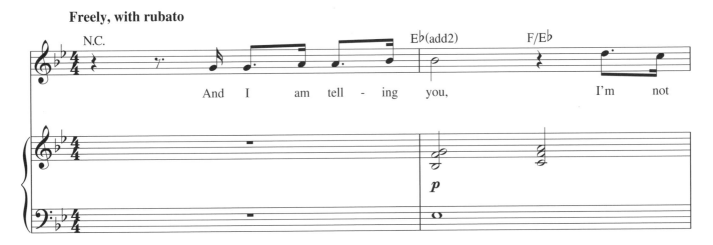

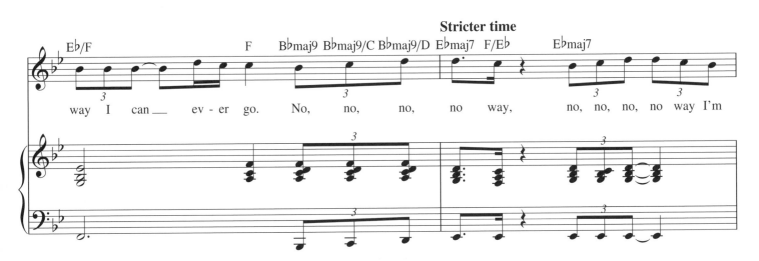

# AS LONG AS HE NEEDS ME

## from the Broadway Musical OLIVER!

Words and Music by
LIONEL BART

**Moderate Ballad, with rubato**

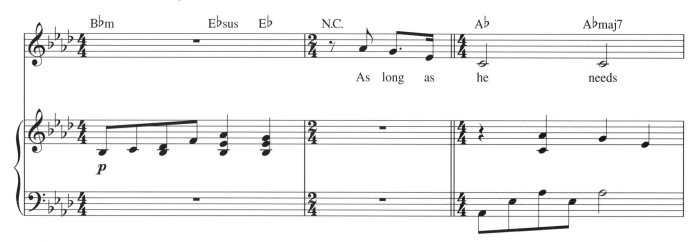

As long as he needs

me, oh yes, he does need me. In spite of

what you see, I'm sure that he needs

# BALI HA'I
## from SOUTH PACIFIC

Lyrics by OSCAR HAMMERSTEIN II
Music by RICHARD RODGERS

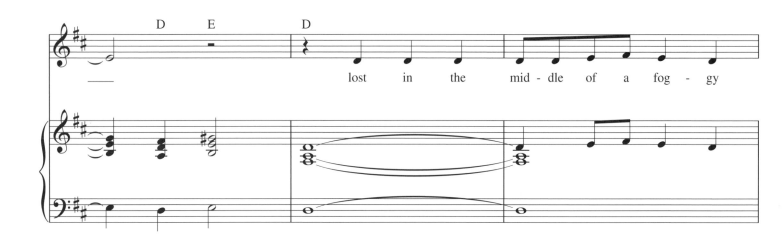

# BEAUTY AND THE BEAST

from Walt Disney's BEAUTY AND THE BEAST: THE BROADWAY MUSICAL

Lyrics by HOWARD ASHMAN
Music by ALAN MENKEN

**Moderate Ballad**

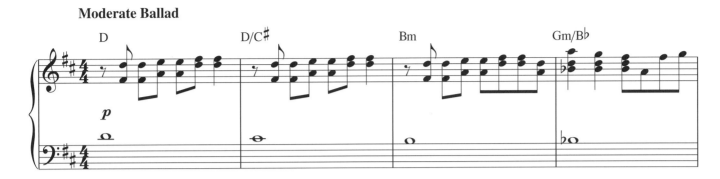

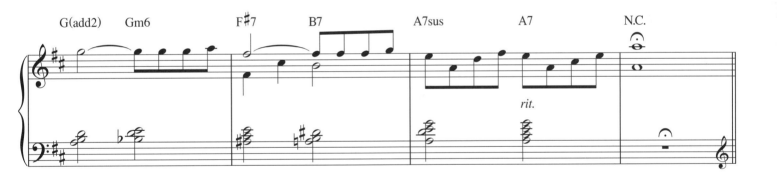

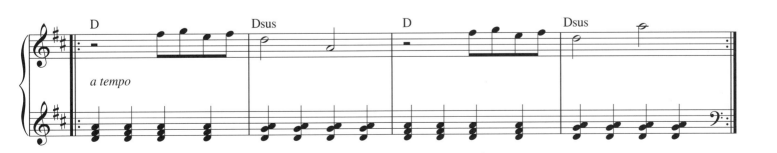

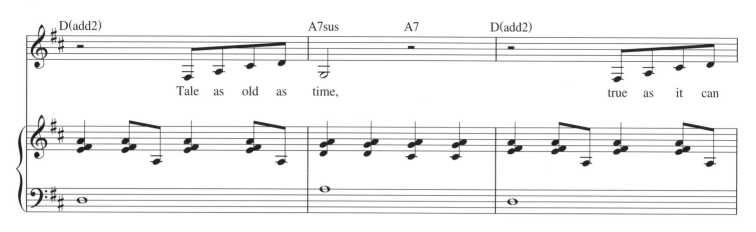

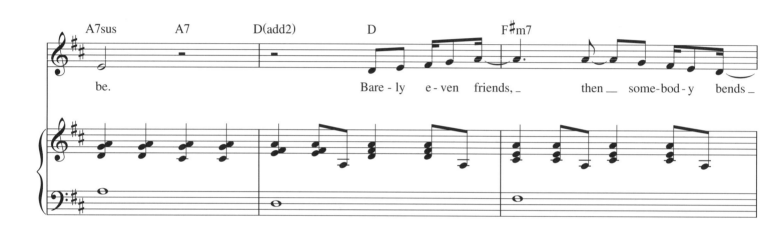

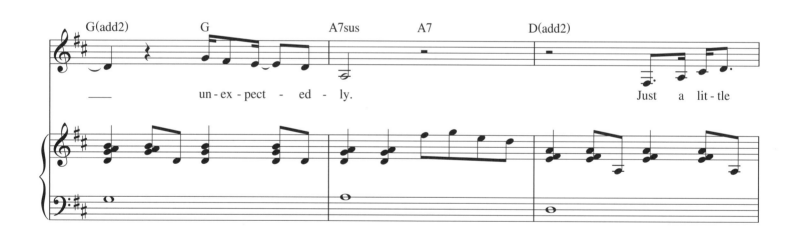

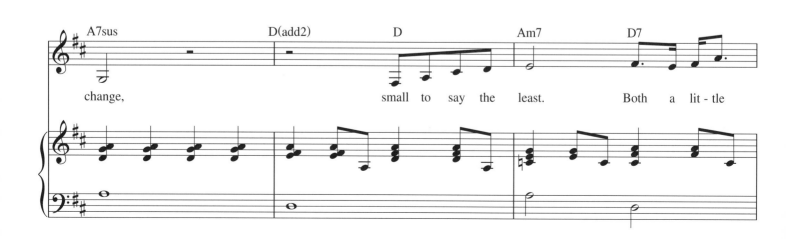

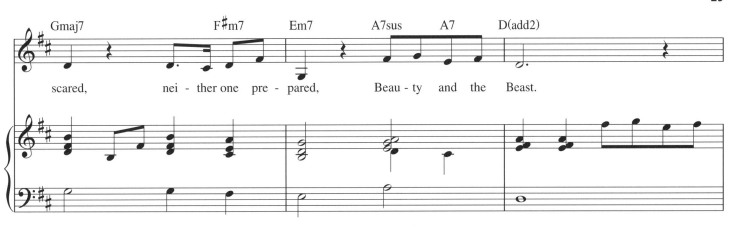

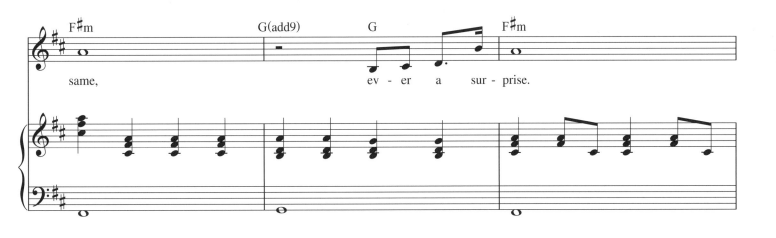

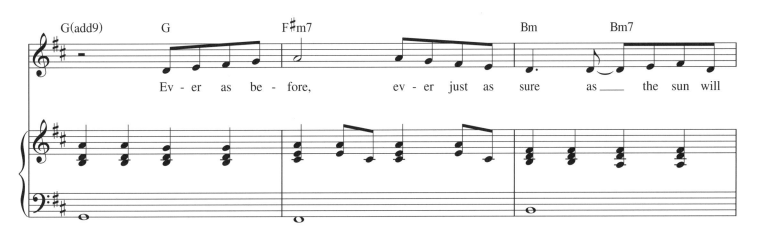

# BIG SPENDER
## from SWEET CHARITY

Music by CY COLEMAN
Lyrics by DOROTHY FIELDS

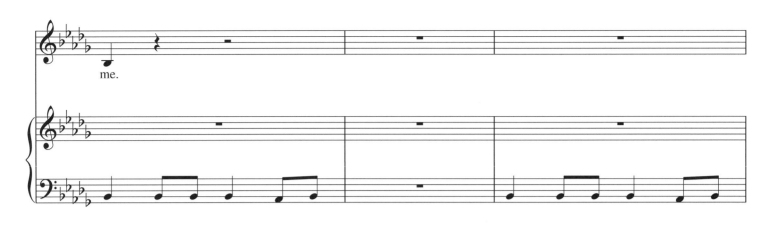

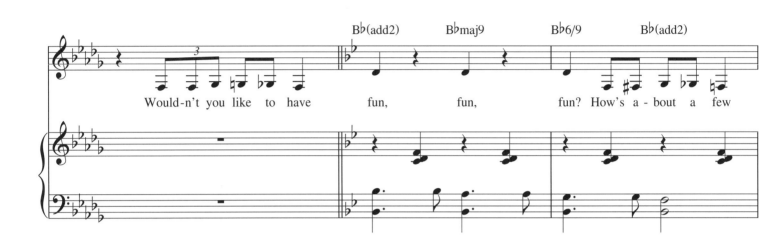

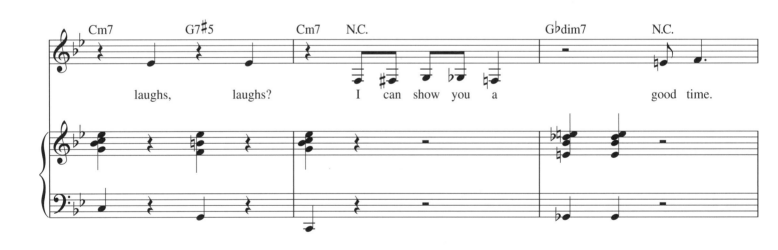

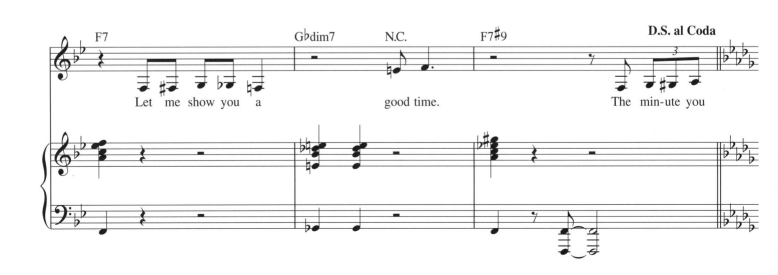

# CABARET
## from the Musical CABARET

Words by FRED EBB
Music by JOHN KANDER

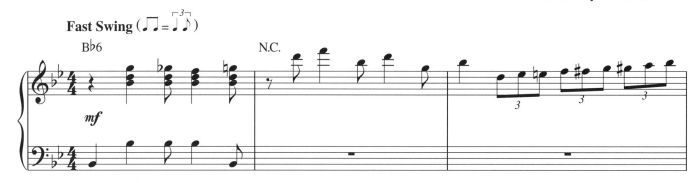

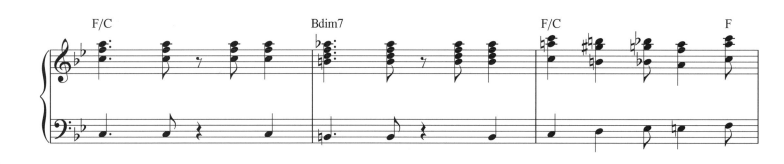

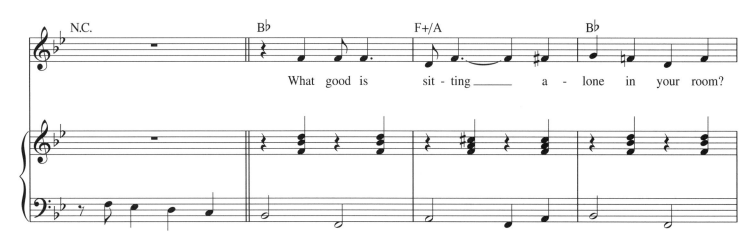

What good is sit-ting ___ a - lone in your room?

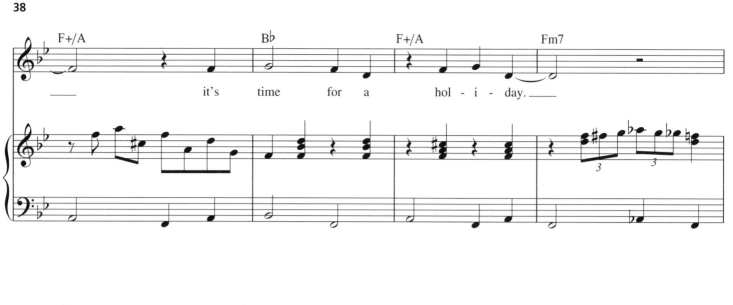

it's time for a hol - i - day. _____

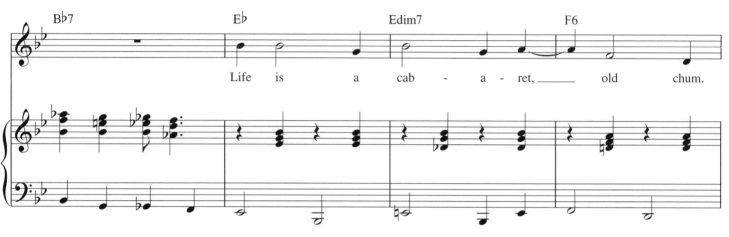

Life is a cab - a - ret, _____ old chum.

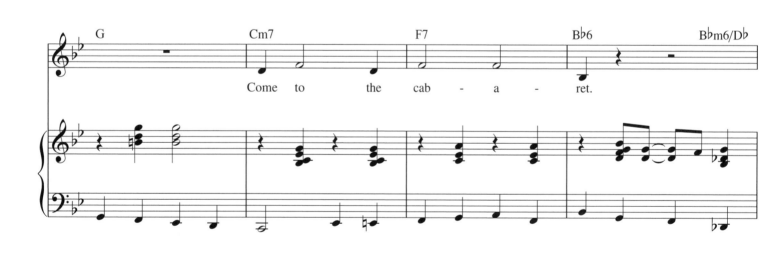

Come to the cab - a - ret.

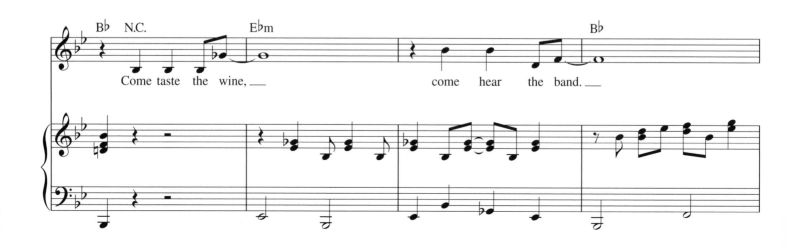

Come taste the wine, ___ come hear the band. ___

Come blow that horn, start cel-e-brat-ing, right this way, your ta-ble's wait-ing. What good's per-mit-ting some proph-et of doom_ to wipe ev-'ry smile a-way? Life is a cab-a-ret, old chum,_

# DEFYING GRAVITY
## from the Broadway Musical WICKED

Music and Lyrics by
STEPHEN SCHWARTZ

**Moderate Ballad**

Some-thing has changed_ with-in _ me,
I'm through ac-cept - ing lim - its

some-thing is not_ the same._
'cause some-one says_ they're so._

I'm through with play - ing by _ the
Some things I can - not change, _ but

rules of some-one el - se's game. _
'til I try, I'll nev - er know.

Too late _ for se-cond guess - ing,
Too long _ I've been a - fraid _ of

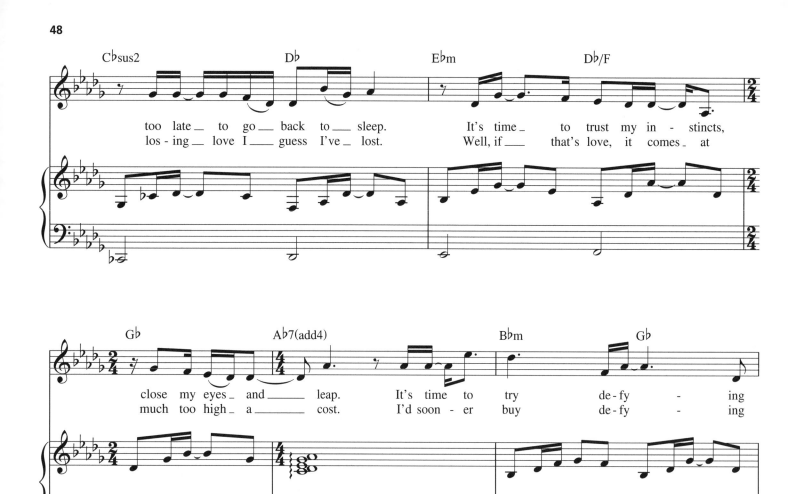

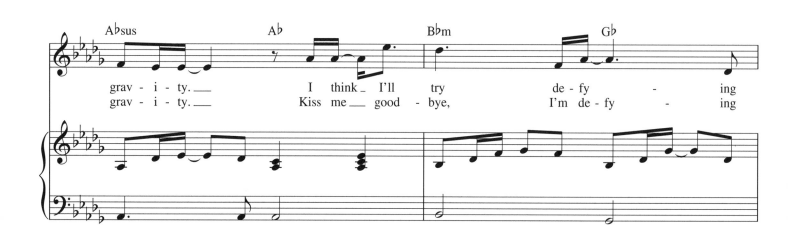

52

# EDELWEISS
## from THE SOUND OF MUSIC

Lyrics by OSCAR HAMMERSTEIN II
Music by RICHARD RODGERS

Gently, with rubato

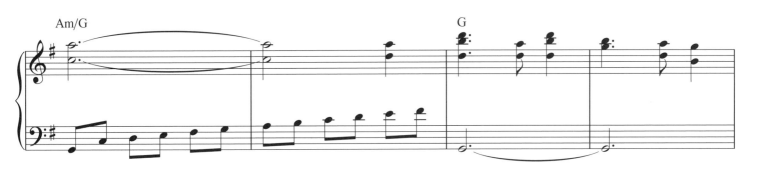

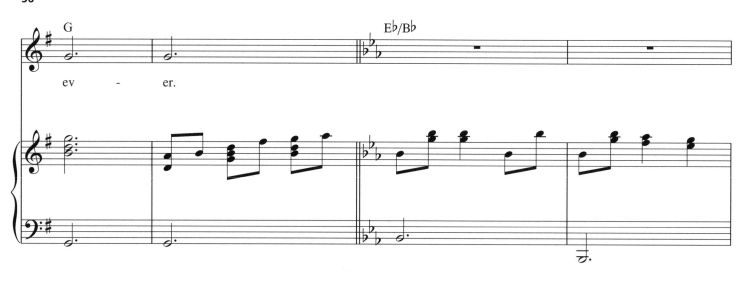

ev - er.

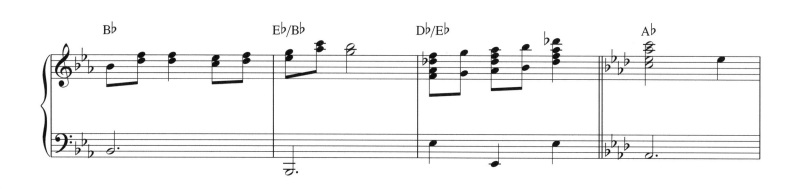

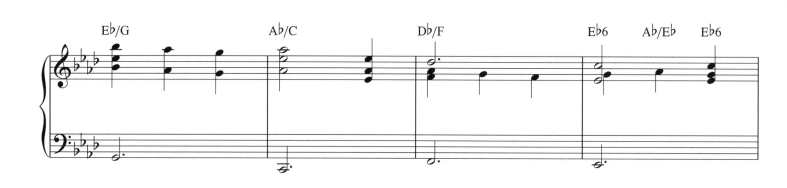

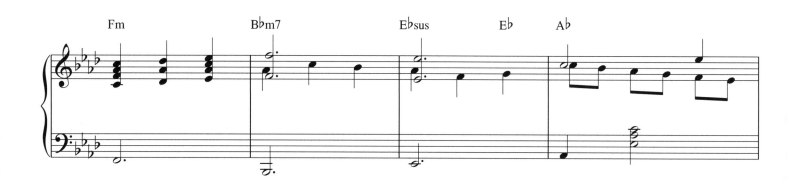

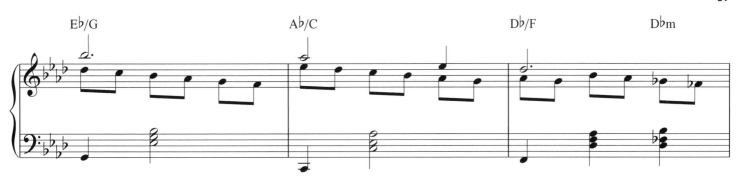

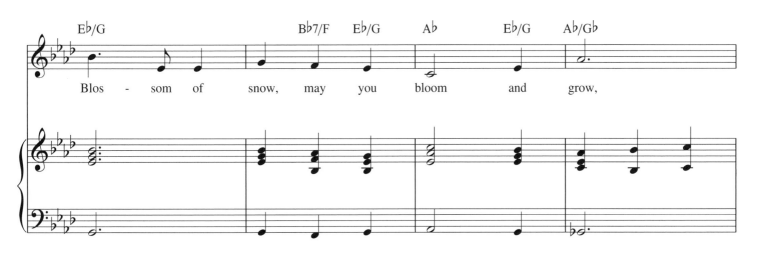

Blos - som of snow, may you bloom and grow,

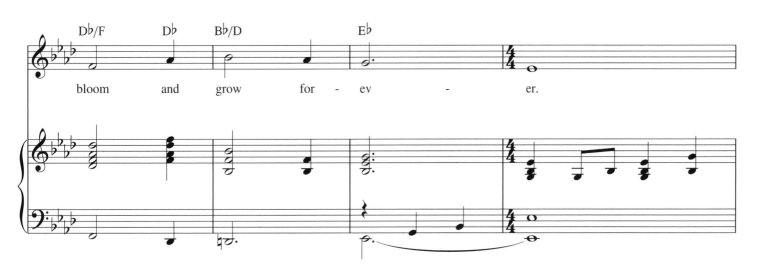

bloom and grow for - ev - er.

# FALLING SLOWLY
## from the Broadway Musical ONCE

Words and Music by GLEN HANSARD
and MARKETA IRGLOVA

**Moderately slow**

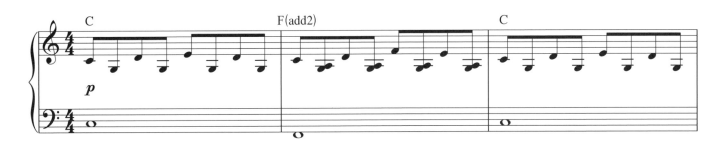

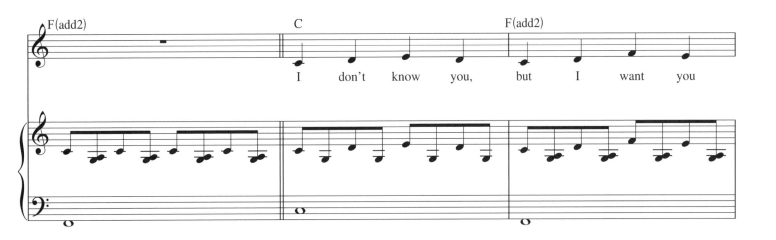

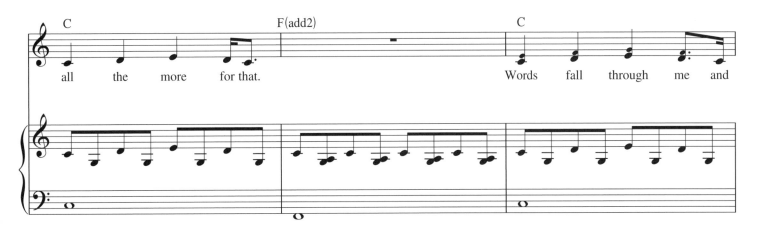

now. _____ Fall - ing slow - ly,

eyes that know me and I can't go back. And

moods that take me and e - rase me, and I'm paint - ed black.

Well, you have suf-fered e - nough and warred with your -

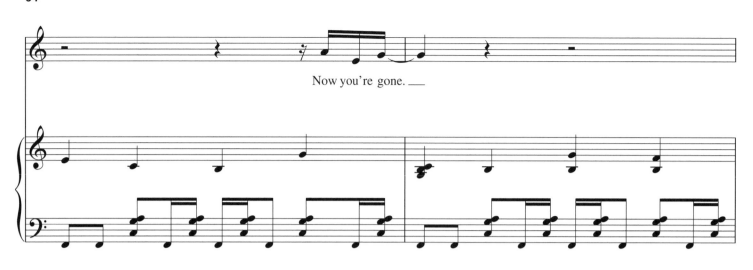

Now you're gone. ___

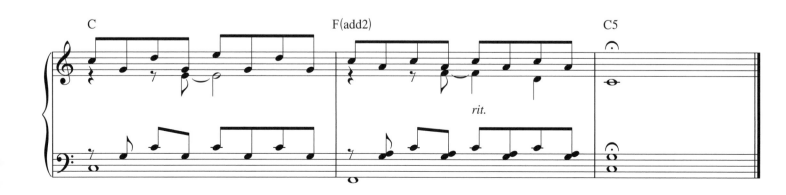

# HEY THERE
## from THE PAJAMA GAME

Words and Music by RICHARD ADLER
and JERRY ROSS

# I DREAMED A DREAM
## from LES MISÉRABLES

Music by CLAUDE-MICHEL SCHÖNBERG
Lyrics by ALAIN BOUBLIL, JEAN-MARC NATEL
and HERBERT KRETZMER

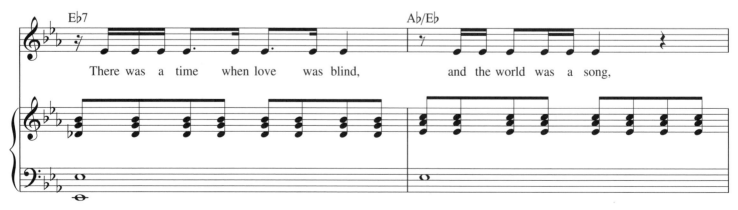

and the song was ex-cit-ing. There was a time it all went wrong.

**A little slower**

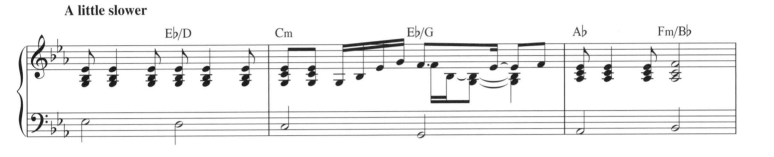

I dreamed a dream in time gone by,

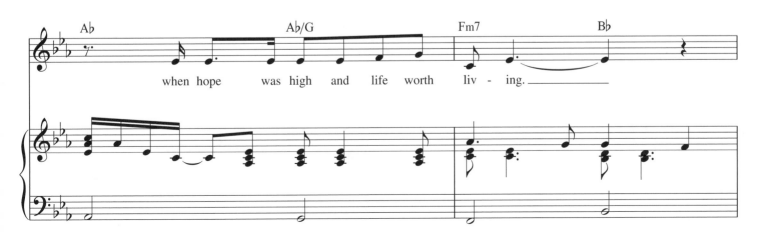

when hope was high and life worth liv-ing. _____

so dif - f'rent from this hell I'm liv - ing, ___ so dif - f'rent now from what it

seemed.

Now life has killed the dream I

**Gently**

dreamed. ____

# I GOT THE SUN IN THE MORNING

## from the Stage Production ANNIE GET YOUR GUN

Words and Music by
IRVING BERLIN

# LOSING MY MIND

## from FOLLIES

Music and Lyrics by
STEPHEN SONDHEIM

The sun __ comes up, I think __ a-bout you. __
The morn - ing ends, I think __ a-bout you. __

The cof - fee cup, I think __ a-bout you. __ I want you so;
I talk __ to friends, I think __ a-bout you. __ And do they know

it's like I'm __ los - ing my mind.
it's like I'm __ los - ing my

# MAYBE THIS TIME
## from the Musical CABARET

Words by FRED EBB
Music by JOHN KANDER

# MEMORY
## from CATS

Music by ANDREW LLOYD WEBBER
Text by TREVOR NUNN after T.S. ELIOT

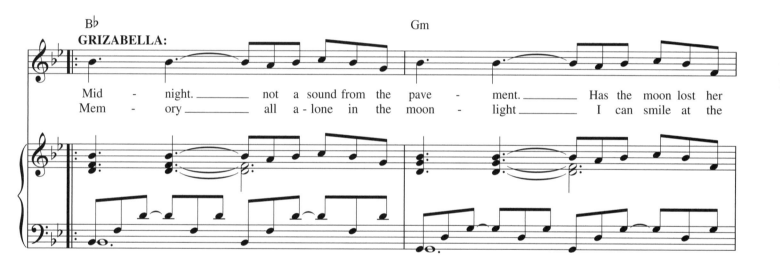

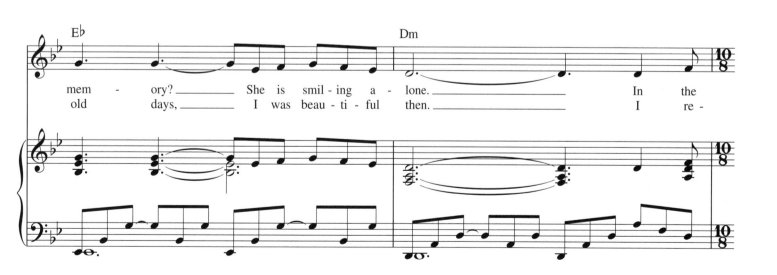

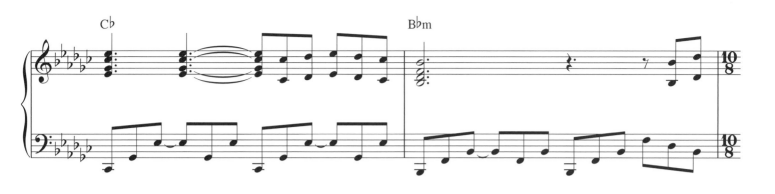

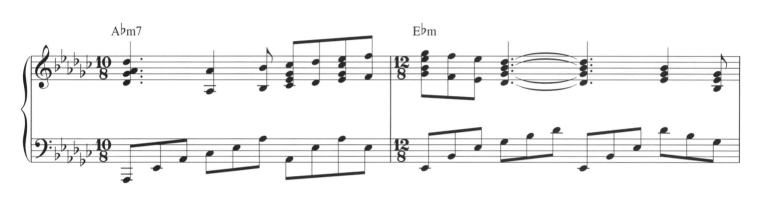

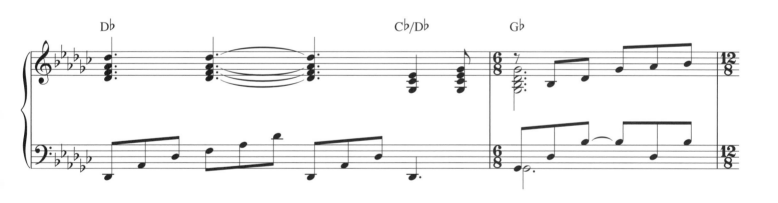

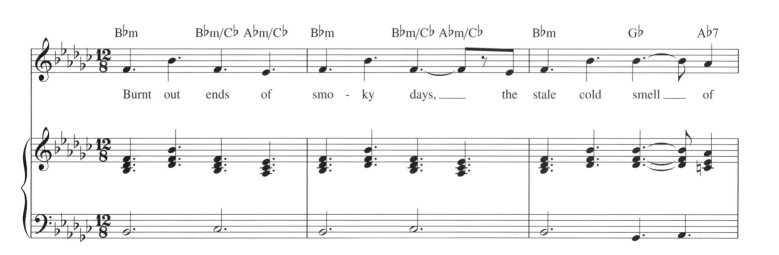

Burnt out ends of smo - ky days, ___ the stale cold smell ___ of

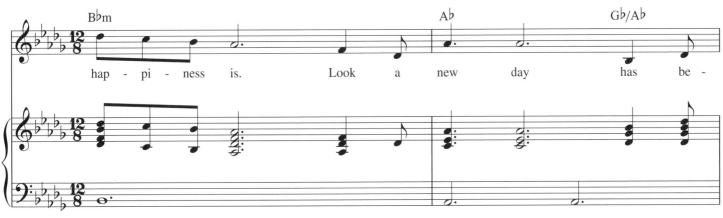

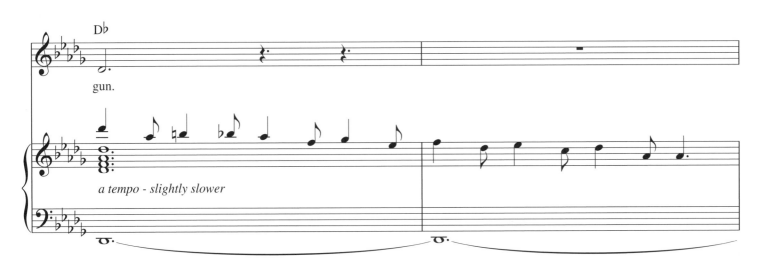

# ON MY OWN

## from LES MISÉRABLES

Music by CLAUDE-MICHEL SCHÖNBERG
Lyrics by ALAIN BOUBLIL, JEAN-MARC NATEL,
HERBERT KRETZMER, JOHN CAIRD
and TREVOR NUNN

**Quickly, with freedom**

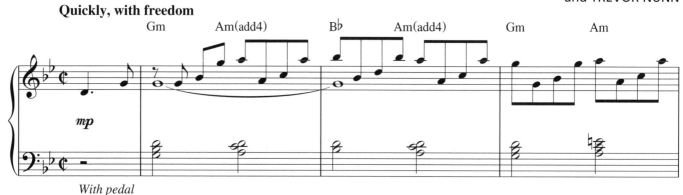

With pedal

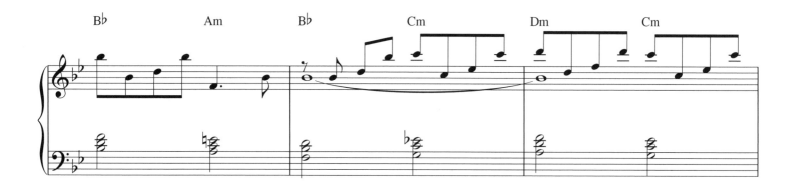

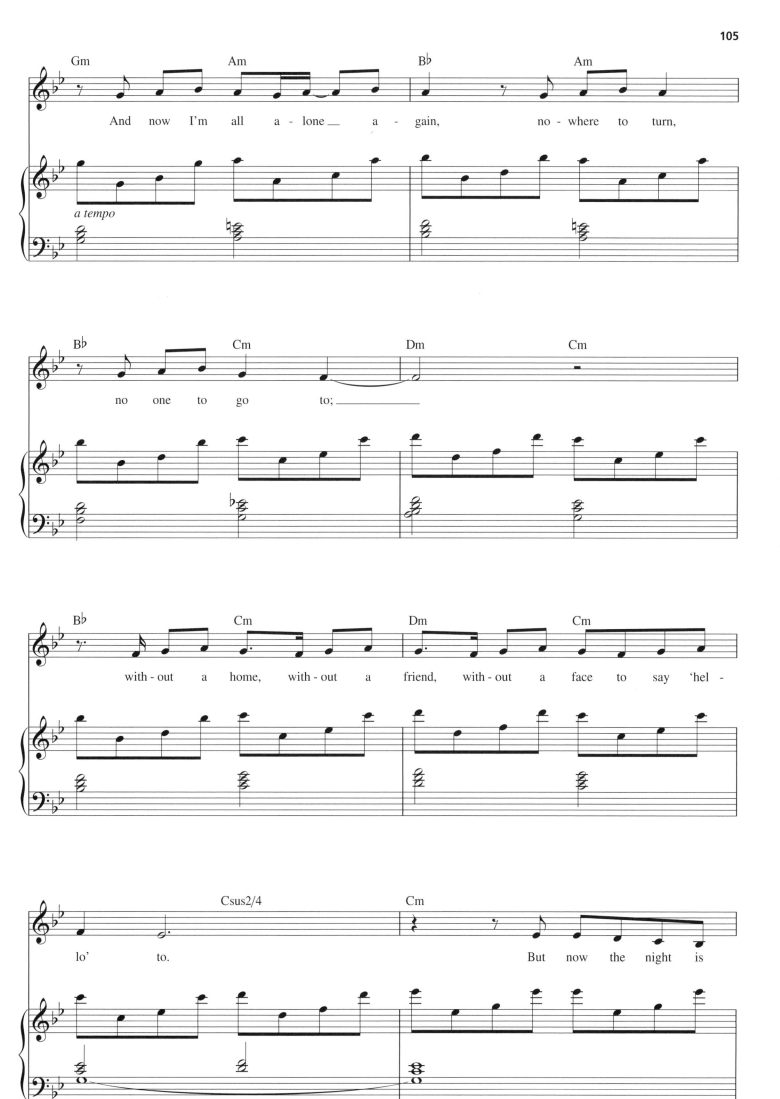

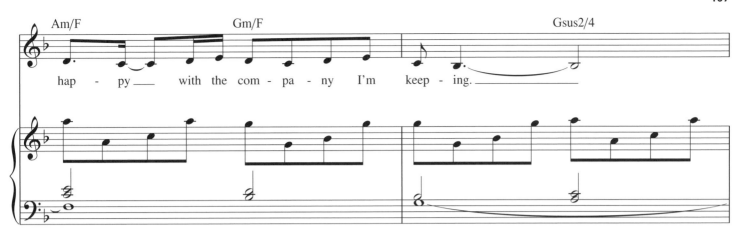

hap - py ___ with the com - pa - ny I'm keep - ing. ___

The cit - y goes to bed, and I can

*rit. e dim.*

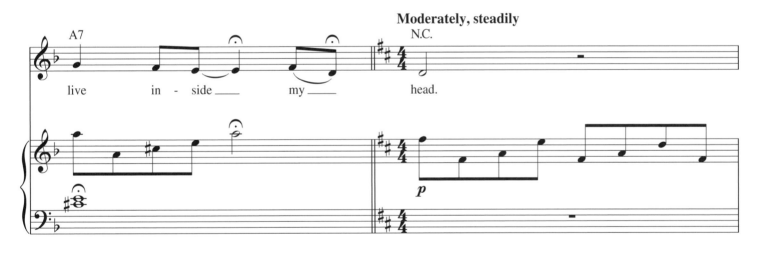

live in - side ___ my ___ head.

**Moderately, steadily**

On my

**Moderately, slower**

turn - ing; ___ a world that's full of hap - pi - ness that I have nev - er known. I love him; ___ I love him; ___ I love him, ___ but on - ly on my ___ own. ___

# OUT HERE ON MY OWN

**from the Broadway Musical FAME**

Music by MICHAEL GORE
Words by LESLEY GORE

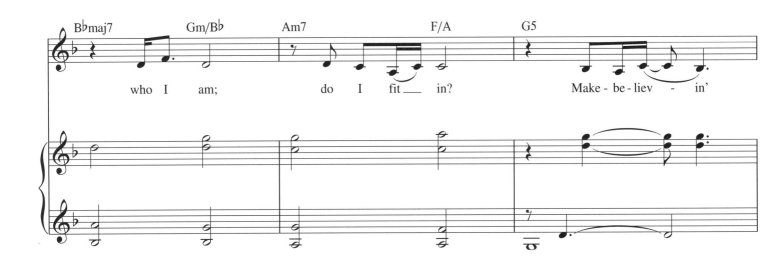

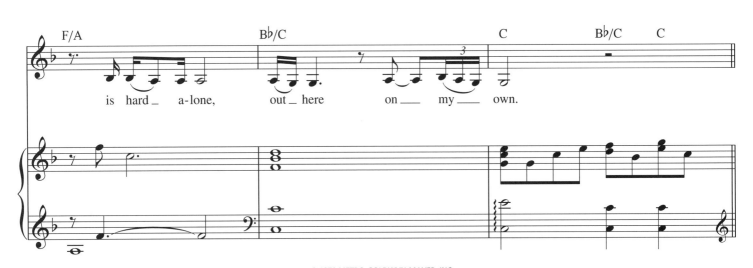

# OVER THE RAINBOW

### from THE WIZARD OF OZ

Music by HAROLD ARLEN
Lyric by E.Y. "YIP" HARBURG

# PEOPLE
## from FUNNY GIRL

Words by BOB MERRILL
Music by JULE STYNE

**Slowly, with freedom**

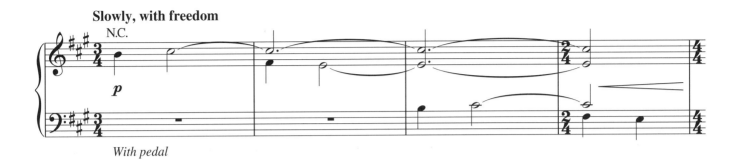

*With pedal*

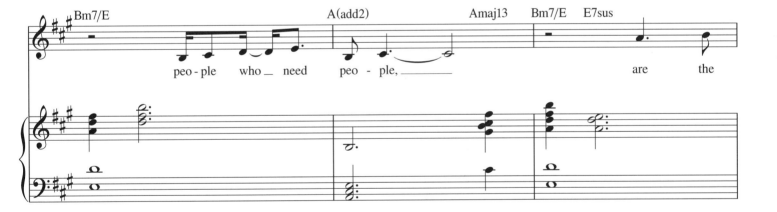

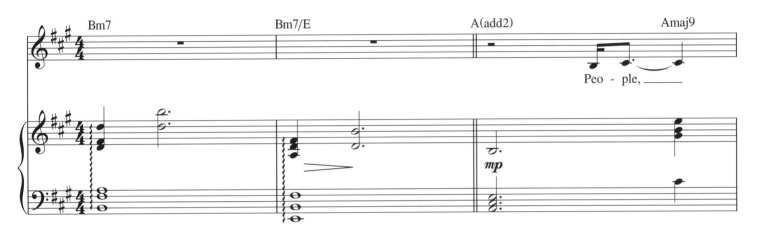

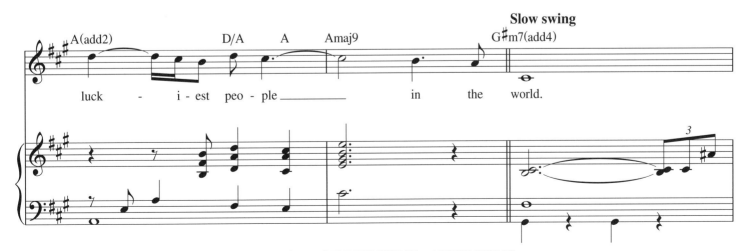

chil - dren          than  chil - dren. _____

Lov - ers _____          are  ver - y  spe - cial  peo - ple; _____

they're  the  luck - i - est  peo - ple _____  in  the

world. _____          With  one  per - son, _____

# SEND IN THE CLOWNS

## from the Musical A LITTLE NIGHT MUSIC

Words and Music by
STEPHEN SONDHEIM

en-trance a-gain _ with my u-su-al flair, sure of my

lines, no one is there. _____

Don't you love farce?
rich?

My fault, I
Is-n't it

fear.
queer,

I thought that you'd ___ want what I ___ want; sor-ry, my
los-ing my tim - ing this _ late in my ca-

# SOMEONE LIKE YOU
## from the Broadway Musical JEKYLL & HYDE

Words and Music by LESLIE BRICUSSE
and FRANK WILDHORN

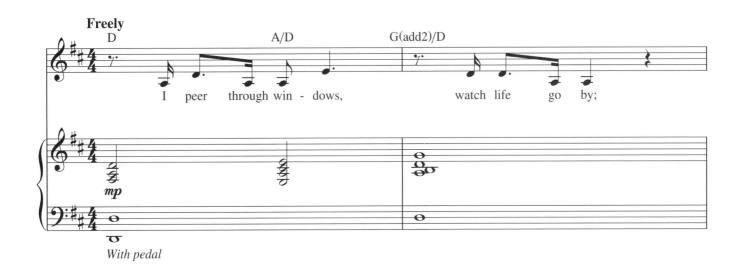

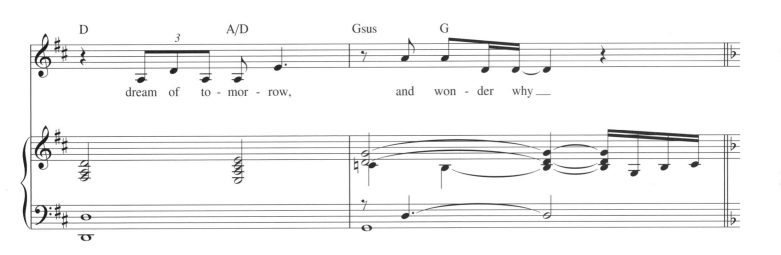

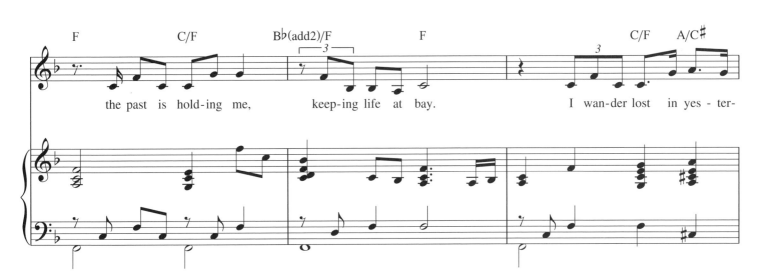

# WHAT I DID FOR LOVE

## from A CHORUS LINE

Music by MARVIN HAMLISCH
Lyric by EDWARD KLEBAN

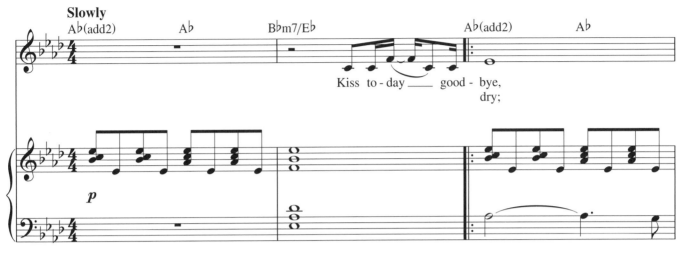

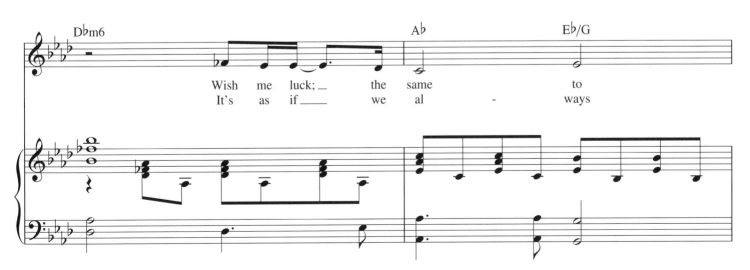